tranquil thoughts

on love

David Baird

tranquil thoughts

on love

MQP

But love is such a mystery,
I cannot find it out;
For when I think I'm best resolv'd,
I then am most in doubt.

Sir John Suckling

Throughout the ages, great writers and thinkers have attempted to solve the mystery of love. Even the Ancients were preoccupied with it—the Egyptians were busily and passionately scrawling love poems onto ornate vases and papyri, and before them the Sumerians and the Babylonians attempted to make sense of their emotions in writing and paintings.

Every great mind has dwelt upon it, from Plato, Martin Luther, Nietzsche, Kierkegaard, Santayana, and

4

Sartre, to Freud and Einstein. Children's stories relate the consequences of love, or lack of love. Novelists, playwrights, poets, and philosophers through the centuries have explored the vicissitudes and pleasures it can bring. Musicians sing of love long into the night. Male or female, no one is immune.

Love is the one emotion that connects human beings across the planet and through the centuries back to the earliest recorded cave dwellers. Everybody, it seems, has attempted to make sense of this elusive condition.

Why do we feel drawn to express the myriad emotions that characterize love? Maybe it is unknowable, unreducible to mere words and images. Perhaps the experience of love feels different for each one of us. The only certainty is that a life without love is a life that is colorless, unfulfilled, and arid. And being in love makes us feel unique and fully alive.

love's seasons

Love finds us when we are ready to change.

Can you think of anyone who is not afraid of change? Yet we all set off on our journey through life in search of love, blissfully unaware that love inevitably changes us. Love demands change, just as nature demands magnificent summer to mature into the richness of fall, to recede into the still quiet of winter, and then burst forth into the excitement of spring to become once more glorious summer. And love, too, has its seasons. When we reach the time in our lives when we are prepared to love and be loved, we must also be prepared and willing to accept the changes love will bring.

invest in your heart

The very
best gift we
can give to
anyone is the experience of love,
either in friendship, in our relationships, or in marriage.
When we give love, we soon discover that we receive more
love in return. "Give a little, receive a lot" may seem a
strange phenomenon to many of us. But love, unlike pennies,
need not be saved to make a fortune, for our investment will
reap loving rewards over and over, throughout the years.

fanning the flames

How can love be explained?

Is it something to do with beauty in the eye of the beholder?
Or the sounds of truth to an attentive ear, or Cupid's arrow
to a willing heart? Take a look around. Evidence of love
surrounds us—history is filled with it. Within each of us is
a glowing spark of love just waiting to be fanned into a full
flame. When love arrives it strikes faster than a thunderbolt
with twice the impact. The flames of love rise and engulf us
and once they have, we will never ever recover.

chemistry

We "make love," but will we ever be able to make love?

In this age of computer technology and genetic engineering, perhaps the time has come for us to reconsider our traditional views on love and ponder it as a neuromolecular constellation. After all, longing, jealousy, desire, bliss, satisfaction, and all the other emotions associated with love are really just expressions of specific neurochemical processes. If we could engineer these processes and come to understand and control them, then "making love" could take on an entirely new meaning.

the spirit of love

It is the
curious nature
of humankind

To love is to take risks.

that a great many of us are prepared only to understand that which we are taught. Everything else is perceived as too great a risk. We convince ourselves that this way of living is satisfactory. How, then, can we ever know love? If we don't, we'll go to the grave brimming over with all the love we never gave—a life spent avoiding the "pains" of love will have been a life that missed out on great happiness. Living this way risks nothing and misses everything. So whatever you do in your lifetime, ensure it is done in the spirit of love.

love's kitchen

Love is a simple but delicious recipe made up of a handful of easy-to-obtain ingredients. There's intimacy, the herb of our natural emotions. It provides the goodness of our feeling towards one

Whether it turns out to be spicy or sweet, tangy or sour is down to the two of you.

another. Intimacy on its own makes for a delicious friendship but if we want to prepare a more substantial repast then we must stock up our Love's Kitchen with trust, compassion, humor, loyalty, and affection. Throw in a dash of passion and soon you'll be cooking up the relationship of your dreams.

Gather the rose of love.

Throughout time, and for all time yet
to come, people have experienced
and always will experience love in
different ways. Perhaps to you love is
like a red, red rose—fragile, beautiful,
and a bit thorny. For some it is like a
box of candies—sweet, comforting,
and indulgent. For others love is like
a shooting star in the night sky—
exciting, awesome, and dangerous.
Each and every one of us has a
different love story to tell.

love is like a ...

healing powers

Use love wisely, and with compassion.

Love is the Band-Aid that reassures a fretting child, a difficult adolescent, a timid student, and an anxious pensioner. We all thrive on love and its incredible healing powers. It comforts those who suffer, provides warmth to those who are alone, and brings hope and encouragement to the sick. It is a refreshing well for those whose hearts are dry and empty.

tell the heart it
needs a reason

There is "love," there is "being in love," and these two are not the same.

One is a form of universal love that seeks to embrace all beings alike and equally. This universal love moves ever outwards, like ripples on a pond, bringing greater peace of mind, acceptance, understanding, and joy to the entire world. The other love is our special love which, when it finds its reason, its moment in time, bathes our entire world in glorious sunshine to bring each of us our greatest joy.

footprints in the

sands of time

Who can ever know where love is going to lead us?

Falling in love is rather like being lost and joining up with a nomadic caravan which we blindly follow out into the desert, leaving behind everything that "was" for everything that is yet to come. From the first step we are changed forever and our life becomes reshaped from that moment onwards.

We are in love, and there is no turning back.

The power of love is boundless and immeasurable.

the great liberator

To try and limit love? The notion is simply ridiculous. It would be like attempting to make the Earth earthless. Love is the great liberator of the mind—it can free us from jealousy, meanness, hatred, and greed. Love can remove the weight of a burdensome past from our shoulders and raise us to a new level of being that is filled with meaning and optimism.

life's lessons

Curiously, it is the good things in life that seem the most difficult to do. There is no difficulty whatsoever in doing bad things. It is far easier to hate than it is to love. It is a ridiculous notion to think that we can be taught to love. How does an infant learn to walk? By walking. How does anyone learn to speak? By speaking. We all find our feet and we all discover our tongues and somewhere in our lives we learn to use our hearts and learn to love by loving.

Learning to love can be the hardest lesson.

"Love is a great beautifier."

Louisa May Alcott

Who has not, at some time, paused to consider whether we are loved because we are beautiful or clever or funny, or if we are all these things because we are loved? Can we ever be certain whether we love the person we love for being who and what they are, or do we love them for who and what we are when we are with them? **Love has its own way of bringing to the surface a part of each of us that would otherwise remain locked away deep within us.**

the beauty within

true value

If you reduce a person to their chemical components, they are worth almost nothing at all. It is love—how much we love others and how much they love us—that gives us our value. Nobody can know what real wealth is until that moment when they have something that money alone just can't buy—Love.

Love brings something priceless into the lives of all who find it.

"Rough diamonds may sometimes be mistaken for worthless pebbles."

Sir Thomas Browne

when love
finds us

We stand our best chance of finding love when we are comfortable with just being ourselves. This way, when love does eventually tap us on the shoulder, as it most certainly will, then we will know that we are being loved for who we really are. Begin here: Get to know yourself, and from that secure foundation love can grow.

together
apart

Where there is true love, there is no separation.

Lovers may not be able to be with one another, or circumstances may prevent them from communicating, yet still they will see and hear each other: in each sunrise and sunset, in birdsong, in the wind at night, in the twinkling stars overhead, in the sound of flowing water, and in the colors of the wildflowers at their feet. Love is everywhere.

let it be ...

When we are in love we spend most of our time thinking of love. We go to bed and spend our sleeping hours dreaming of love. We experience emotions we have never felt before, and live in fear of losing love. If we wish to maintain the wonderful mysteriousness of it, then maybe we should not be tempted to hold our love up to such severe scrutiny. It would be better if we were to just "let it be."

the poetry
of love

Ah! what is love! It is a pretty thing,
As sweet unto a shepherd as a king.

Robert Greene

If love has a nature then what words can we use to describe it? Is it actually possible to know love, to comprehend it, let alone describe it? We can utter the words "I love you" or tell the world "I am in love." Love leaves us dumbfounded or babbling like babies; it is totally beguiling. Perhaps that is why poets have the lead role in its interpretation.

eternity

love and the movement of time

Wait for love
  and time will pass slowly;
Fear love
  and love's moment will pass you
by all too swiftly,
Never to return.
Grieve for your lost love
  and time will weigh you down.
Rejoice when you find true love
  and it will last for eternity.

can love endure?

Time takes on another meaning for those of us who are in love. How can love endure? If the object of our love is beauty, does not beauty fade with time? Can we come to know someone too well? What becomes of love when the beauty, the discovery, the fun, and the laughter dry up? In love every moment is a wonderful new revelation if we can bring ourselves to love the other person just for being who they are.

the magic triangle

If one side of our triangle is intimacy, another is formed from passion. If we add commitment as the third side, our triangle becomes complete. Complete love with all the satisfaction of friendship, the thrill of romance, and the peace of mind of commitment— this is the love that every heart willingly seeks and longs to receive.

love at first sight

"Who ever loved that loved not at first sight?"

As You Like It, William Shakespeare

We open our eyes and are overwhelmed. Something, a new feeling—unexpected, unsought, unknown—takes complete possession of us and suddenly, to our amazement, we find we are filled with joy and more conscious than ever before. This is love at first sight! And it will remain with us for the rest of our lives.

love story

We could build a tower to the stars with what has
been written in the name of love. We could fill
every quiet moment with the talk of love: spiritual
love, love in its highest form, the music of the
spheres ... the cosmic dance between lovers and
their passages through every stage of separation
and union. Each of us desires to be part
of some sacred love story;
to merge in love and discover
that place where divinity
and humanity fully embrace
one another.

ever-expanding love

We often hear in song lyrics that someone's love is deeper than the ocean or higher than the highest mountain. This extraordinary thing called love can be as big as the entire universe and still be capable of expanding further; yet it can also be compressed into a grain of sand, a fragrance, a droplet, or a sigh. The most powerful sentence in the world has the greatest meaning despite its brevity.

It is "I love you."

When two one-winged angels meet...

The most wonderful feelings in the world are the moments when you feel your heart smiling for the very first time, or you experience the truth of a lover's kiss. It could be a first embrace and the feeling of two hearts beating as one, or the sound of three little words whispered into your ear. The spirit soars, everything finds its meaning, the heart opens and happiness enters.

never forgotten

Everyone, at some time, experiences the feeling that their love has been misplaced. It can be frightening, but there is a cure. Create some time and space. When you close your eyes and think of love, what do you see? What can you hear? Each of us has the power to rekindle our love. To succeed we must look at things as we used to look at them, for while the memory of material things soon becomes overwhelmed, the memory of true love remains eternal.

Everything is touched by love

We must always leave room in our life for love; it is the stimulus for everything that is good. True love is the harbor for our warmest affections. It puts pain into partings and joy into reunions, color in the cheeks, and a spring into every step. It can uncap the deepest well of our secret emotions and ignite the fuse of our greatest sensations. When two people are in love they should use each other well, for love is mankind's truest pleasure and nature's greatest truth.

nature's truth

from the hilltop

How will we know when we are in love?

Will we recognize the signs? Suddenly, all reality
will become even more exciting than our dreams.
Suddenly, we will understand the meaning of
serendipity. We shall have stars in our eyes and
a spring in our step. We will begin to write
letters to our lover not knowing what to say and
we will post them before we know what it was
that we wrote. We will feel fulfilled and
somehow united, joined from a point deep down
within us, so deep that it does not have a name
and has never been seen by the human eye.

love will tell

Love is the greatest influence there is upon who we are and how we are defined by others. You can always tell those whose lives have been touched by love. Within them sits an inexhaustible magical spring from which love bubbles to the surface. The fact that these loving people are willing to love us too makes them extraordinary and special in our eyes.

They teach us that no matter how great it is to give love, it is even more wonderful to receive it.

love does not come without pain

It is different to the pain that exists prior to love—feeling starved of affection, shriveling up in a cold world. When love enters our life, the nature of pain changes. Suddenly, we cannot bear the pain of being apart, even for a moment—we love someone so much that it hurts. The greatest pain of all is surely to love someone and to never find the courage to let them know.

heart's capacity

I love to sleep, I love to dream, and I love to wake. When I wake I love all that I see around me—each particle of dust trapped in the rays of the sun, each molecule of air that I breathe, the people I encounter, every grain of sand and the world contained within it, the birds in the trees, those who are with me and those who are not, the colors, the sounds, the smells, and the tastes. I love this day, this universe and all things in it. How much love is that?

what do we love?

When we love someone, we love everything about them: all those irritating little habits, the chaos they create, their jealous moments, their desires, attitudes, moods, and requirements. Over time these same things could become the irritations that drive us apart; but if we see them from the outset and always remember them as the qualities we fell in love with, then even the loudest snorers in the world will still be able to wake up next to their life partners.

what we
know now

Human beings are wonderful, complicated, and fickle creatures.

From the moment we can utter a few words and propel ourselves, we rush out into the world in a constant state of "I want—I want—." And we shall continue in this manner for the remainder of our days, searching for that essential something that we think we always wanted.

Until, that is, after tearing about blindly in every direction, the great day comes when we discover that our search should be turned inwards.

And when it is, we discover that love was in our heart all along and that love is everything we never knew we always wanted.

Before I found love I used to close my eyes and see my heart—just my heart, and a big black void. Nothing more. Just a tiny insignificant organ suspended there in time and space. Then love entered my life, and now I see a heart where the black void had once been and through its windows I can see all of mankind, and all of nature. And as I draw that heart into myself and open my eyes, I can see in the mirror that the void was me and that it has been filled with love.

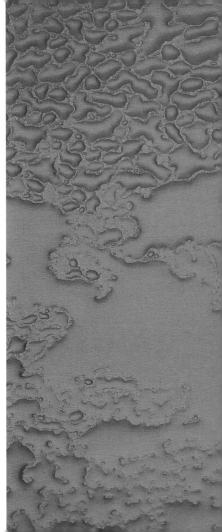

a meditation

loving-kindness

Where there is hatred, there is also somewhere to be found its opposite—love.

Where there is resentment, malevolence, pride, or arrogance, there is also love. It may be in short supply, but like the grit in an oyster shell, it will finally triumph as a precious pearl. Love always chooses the path of goodwill and kindness. Imagine a world smothered with so much loving-kindness that it would be impossible for anyone to harbor bad feelings, negative thoughts, or injurious intentions.

together forever

When our hearts intertwine and we become as one, we move forward together, our hearts committed to each other. And perhaps, as we get older, the passion may dwindle, yet the commitment and intimacy remains. In these twilight years we can still allow the sweet memories of our passion to rise up within us, and in doing so we will fall in love with our partner over and over again.

turn on love's tap

Do you feel that you shy away from love and loving? That you'd like to be that warm, generous human being you admire? It's ever so easy—it's just a case of crossing that self-imposed line. From the waking moment, become that loving person and feel the change within yourself. Then allow others into your space and observe how their attitude towards you also undergoes a transformation. Soon, through interaction, you will find that you are not pretending and that in fact you never were.

You will simply have turned on the tap that allows your love to flow through your own life and the lives of others.

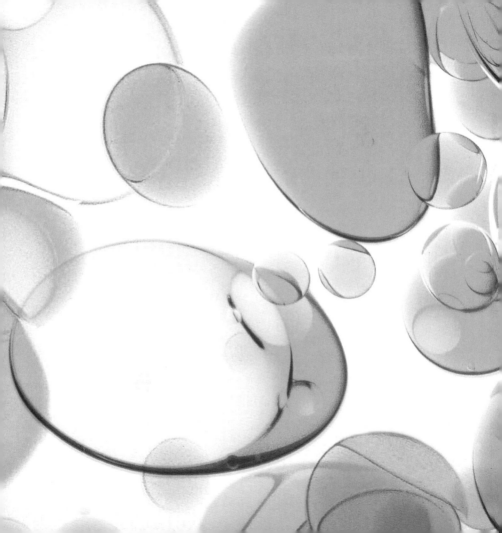

love can't be packaged

Love is unique and can manifest itself in wild and unpredictable ways. Some may discover Mariachi troubadours serenading under their balcony. Others hurtle over waterfalls in a barrel to express their affection. While it is always pleasant to receive a box of chocolates, some long-stemmed roses, or a diamond, love may take some getting used to if your new partner's sense of romance results in a gorilla-gram arriving at your office.

The essential thing is not to shy away from expressing your love. A poem that has been written by you is always a perfect standby when you can't lay your hands on a barrel.

two souls in the
balance

To remain perfectly in balance, yin needs yang, light needs dark, and good needs bad.

Cast your mind back to childhood. Remember being alone in a playground, sitting on the seesaw, silently longing for someone to get on the other end, and how good it felt when somebody did? Everything in life is held in delicate balance by the power of light opposing the dark. Each needs the other to exist. And we are scarcely different. Although we can "exist" alone without love, don't we owe it ourselves to take up the empty seat on the seesaw?

love's garden

Young love, new love is as fragile and full of potential as a
newly planted garden. It must be nurtured and constantly
attended if it is to develop and thrive. As the new roots
begin to take hold, they must be regularly watered with
sweet loving words, and composted with affection.
Destructive weeds will need to be held back with constant
affirmation and tilling of the soul. With the correct care and
a brave heart, your garden of love will continue to flourish
come rain or shine to be enjoyed daily, gazed upon enviously
by passers-by, and emulated
by generations to come.

"When love and skill work together, expect a masterpiece." John Ruskin

the nature of
love in others

When people fall in love, nothing anyone can do is going to change the outcome.

To try and tame a person's love makes no more sense than attempting to put a leash on the fiercest tornado and take it for a walk out of harm's way. If love survives all the twists and turns and ups and downs then you can relax and be grateful. Meanwhile, would it not be better just to remain supportive and close at hand for the other, whether the love lasts or not?

the power of love

Where there is love, there is still hope.

Love is the key to everything in life—even to life itself. Love is capable of moving mountains, it can lead to incredible feats of strength and human endurance, and can save lives. In extreme danger, people who love each other will never give up while there is a glimmer of a chance. Love's impulses are so strong that mothers have been known to lift vehicles from on top of their children. We should never underestimate the power of love.

magnetic attraction

With magnets, like poles repel each other and opposite poles attract. The magnetism of love is the same only more profound. When two people who are too alike enter a relationship, often they see too many of their own traits in the other

When two people are attracted to each other, there is a form of magnetism involved.

and this begins to repel them. The attraction is strongest in a relationship in which one is able to provide the opposite "pole," perhaps by providing sympathy or forgiveness, tolerance, admiration, belief, or appreciation for the other person.

love is enough

Love is the purest form of magic and goodness there is and when we feel it we should never be frightened to share it—to scatter it onto the winds to be carried to the four corners of the earth—and the seeds of it should be sown by us everywhere we go. The world needs all the love it can get, and even the tiniest speck can turn a living hell into a peaceful heaven. Love is all we have, and it's the only way that each can help the other.

Love is enough.

Suddenly, love was everywhere

creating trust

Imagine encountering a mistreated horse. The poor animal has been overworked and regularly beaten until it has become angry, and mistrustful of all who approach it. But the loving heart knows that with patience all that anger can be drawn from the beast and through gentleness, care, and comforting, trust can be re-established. With love, ill-will stands no chance at all and is soon warded off. The broken spirit becomes the most loyal of friends and both are deserving of each other's love.

There is no ill when there is love.

95

words of love

While contemplating love is important and to be encouraged, if we're not careful we can soon fall into the trap of missing out on the real thing that is out there somewhere just waiting for us. Perhaps it would be better to contemplate love less in terms of words and attempt to get into contact with the feelings of love by recognizing when the conditions feel right and by getting out there and experiencing it instead of thinking about it.

All of Nature's gifts are born from love.

The vines becoming heavy with fruit and the grains rising up in the fields—Nature's love is Earth's life renewed. The desert shows its love of rain by turning into a wonderful blooming garden. The ocean shows its love of the moon by becoming still and glasslike and reflecting that love. We, too, are loved and free to run out into the wilderness and to commune with Nature, for our love is Nature's life renewed.

And Nature's love of us is like that of a mother for her child.

a mother's love

love is the core of existence

Astonishing as it may seem, there are things about ourselves that we will never discover until we are in love. Each new day in a loving relationship teaches us a little more about ourselves: that we talk in our sleep, perhaps, or that our singing voice, overheard in the shower, is considered "lovely." It could be the discovery that sushi is not to our taste while scuba diving on the Great Barrier Reef is. We discover we can be braver than we ever imagined at times when our partner is in danger. And perhaps the nicest discovery of all is that we're not half as bad as we originally imagined ourselves to be.

do we fall or are we pushed?

In truth, most of us tend to step into love, for that is generally the way it happens.

You go alone through life and then someone draws a line on the ground in front of you and the dilemma is whether to cross it or not. Some of us turn and walk away; others will be egged on by friends or other forces and pushed across it. But mostly when we reach that line, we gather up all our senses, our being and our baggage, and step across it willingly in the hope that we will never return again to the other side from whence we came.

split second

"It is wrong to think that love comes from long companionship and persevering courtship. Love is the offspring of spiritual affinity and unless that affinity is created in a moment, it will not be created for years or even generations."

Kahlil Gibran

love's
philosophy

THE fountains mingle with the river
And the rivers with the ocean,
The winds of heaven mix for ever
With a sweet emotion;
Nothing in the world is single,
All things by a law divine
In one another's being mingle:
Why not I with thine?

See the mountains kiss high heaven,
And the waves clasp one another;
No sister-flower would be forgiven
If it disdain'd its brother;
And the sunlight clasps the earth,
And the moonbeams kiss the sea;
What are all these kissings worth,
If thou kiss not me?   Percy Bysshe Shelley

love is the key

Love is the doorway of hope through which we expect to find the daylight of a new and better life.

To find love we must come to accept our past and have belief in our future.

To unlock it we must nurture within ourselves the capacity to love others, particularly those who feel that love has no part in their lives. To enter through it we must understand that sometimes the love we seek can only exist in fairy tales and that ahead of us lies the real love—the kind of love that makes us feel real, human, and fully alive.

Published by MQ Publications Limited
12 The Ivories
6–8 Northampton Street
London N1 2HY
Tel: +44 (0)20 7359 2244 / Fax: +44 (0)20 7359 1616
e-mail: mail@mqpublications.com
website: www.mqpublications.com

Text © 2003 David Baird
Cover image: Grace Carlon, Flowers & Foliage
Interior images: © Digital Vision

ISBN: 1-84072-467-6

10 9 8 7 6 5 4 3 2 1

Printed in China

Note on the CD

The music that accompanies this book has been specially commissioned from composer David Baird. Trained in music and drama in Wales, and on the staff of the Welsh National Opera & Drama company, David has composed many soundtracks for both the theater and radio.

The CD can be played quietly through headphones while relaxing or meditating on the text. Alternatively, lie on the floor between two speakers placed at equal distances from you. Try to center your thoughts, and allow the soundtrack to wash over you and strip away the distracting layers of the outside world.